Bees

Bees

Mary Ann McDonald

THE CHILD'S WORLD®

Published in the United States of America by The Child's World®
P.O. Box 326
Chanhassen, MN 55317-0326
800-599-READ
www.childsworld.com

Project Manager Mary Berendes
Editor Katherine Stevenson, Ph.D.
Designer Mary Berendes

Photo Credits
ANIMALS ANIMALS © David M. Dennis: 2
ANIMALS ANIMALS © Donald Specker: 29 (main)
© Annie Griffiths Belt/CORBIS: 20
© Christoph Burki/Stone: 10 (bottom)
© Clive Druett; Papilio/CORBIS: 10 (top)
© David Maitland/Taxi: 9
© Gerry Ellis/Minden Pictures: 16 (bottom)
© Keren Su/The Image Bank: 6
© Konrad Wothe/Minden Pictures: 19
© Lynda Richardson/CORBIS: 15, 29 (inset)
© Mark Moffett/Minden Pictures: 26
© Paul A. Souders/CORBIS: 30
© Paul Beard/PhotoDisc: 16 (top)
© Paul McCormick/The Image Bank: 24
© Peter Johnson/CORBIS: 13
© Royalty-Free/CORBIS: 23
© Scott T. Smith/CORBIS: cover

Library of Congress Cataloging-in-Publication Data
McDonald, Mary Ann.
Bees / by Mary Ann McDonald.
p. cm.—(Naturebooks series)
Contents: Meet the bee!—What do bees look like?—Where do bees live?—How do
bees protect themselves?—Do bees live together?—How do new colonies form?—What
do bees eat?—How do honey bees communicate?.
ISBN 1-56766-611-6 (lib. bdg. : alk. paper)
1. Bees—Juvenile literature. [1. Bees.] I. Title. II. Naturebooks (Chanhassen, Minn.)
QL565.2.M36 2003
595.79'9—dc21
2002151470

On the cover...

Front cover: This honeybee is pollinating a cosmos flower.
Page 2: These honeybees are very busy in their hive.

Table of Contents

It's a warm June day, and your mom surprises you with a picnic lunch out in the yard. She brings out some of your favorite foods: a peanut butter sandwich, carrots, cookies, and milk. Next she brings out a special treat to put on your sandwich, honey. As you eat, a yellow and black **insect** buzzes around the garden from one flower to another. Your mother tells you that this little insect makes the honey you are eating! What busy little insect makes this delicious sweet treat? It's a bee!

What Do Bees Look Like?

Bees belong to a group of animals called insects. All insects have six legs and a body divided into three areas. The front area is the head. The middle area is the chest, or **thorax**. The back area is the belly, or **abdomen**. Many insects also have two sets of wings.

All bees are black or brown and are covered with hair. Many of them also have white, yellow, or orange on their faces or bodies. Bees have a very long, pointed tongue. They use their tongue for sipping a liquid called **nectar** from flowers. Bees also have a sharp, hollow stinger on the end of their abdomen.

From close up, you can easily see this bee's body parts. ⇒

Bees live everywhere in the world except Antarctica. That's because Antarctica is too cold to grow the flowers and plants that bees need to stay alive. The best-known kind, or **species**, of bee in the world is the *honeybee*. It gets its name from the sticky honey it makes from the nectar of flowers.

⇐ *Top*: Here you can see a bumblebee as it collects nectar from a flower in England.

Bottom: This carpenter bee is feeding on the nectar of a flower.

Killer bees are relatives of the honeybee. They live in warm areas of the world, such as Mexico and Africa. Killer bees got their name because they can be very dangerous. They attack in large numbers, which means lots of stings for anything that comes near them or their home. Killer bees become angry for almost any reason—even strange noises and smells!

These African honeybees, also known as killer bees, ⇒ have gathered on a tree stump in Botswana. The bees will build their hive inside the stump.

How Do Bees Protect Themselves?

Bees protect themselves with their sharp stingers. When a bee stings something, special sacs in the bee's body pump out a poison. The poison travels through the stinger and into the victim's body. Honeybees have stingers with tiny points sticking out called **barbs**. These barbs get stuck in the victim's skin. To get away, the bee must tear itself away from its stinger. By tearing its stinger off, the bee makes a hole in its body. Soon the bee dies from its wound, but it has done its job of protecting the hive.

Here you can see a bee stinging a man's arm. ⇒

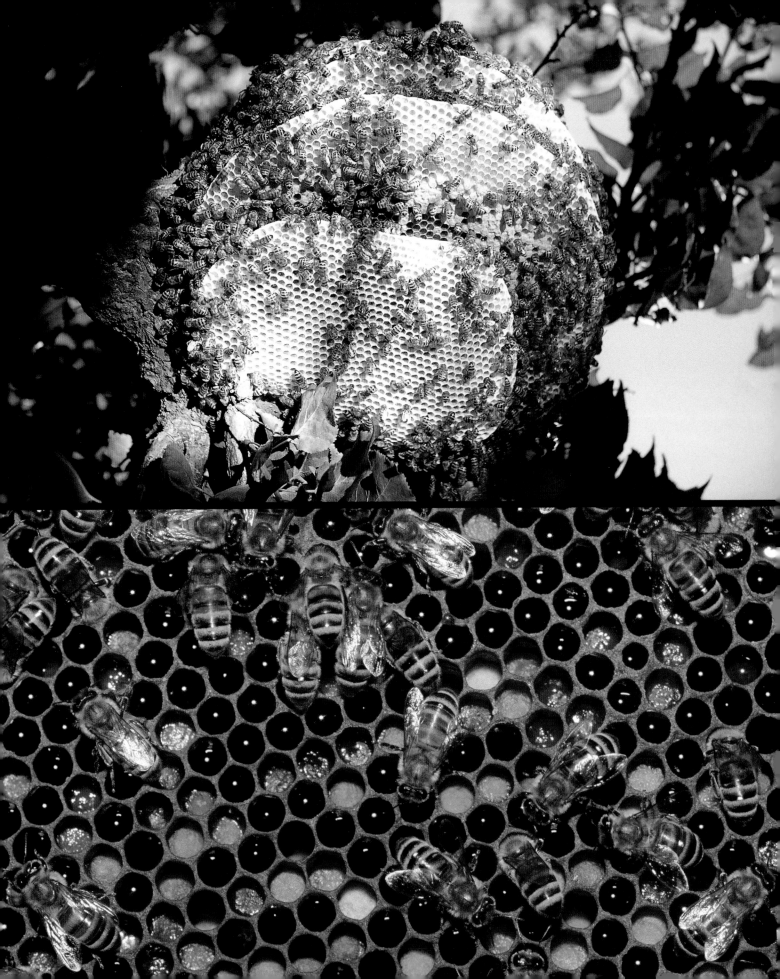

Many species of bees live alone. They are called *solitary bees*. Most solitary bees dig holes in the ground. They line these holes with mud, leaves, or small parts of plants. They use the holes for resting and escaping from danger.

Other bees, such as honeybees and *bumblebees*, live in huge groups. A large group of insects living together is called a **colony**. Some bee colonies are huge—more than 50,000 bees! Big colonies like this are called **hives**. Hives are made up of thousands of little rooms called **combs**. Combs are used for raising baby bees and storing honey.

⇐ *Top*: This honeybee hive is in a tree.

Bottom: You can clearly see the combs of this honeybee colony.

Colonies are made up mostly of worker bees. Worker bees are females who can't lay eggs. Instead, they spend their whole lives working hard. They clean the hive, feed the young bees, and build the combs. Worker bees also protect the colony and hunt for food.

The most important bee in the colony is the queen bee. She is the largest bee, and she only has one job—to lay eggs! Worker bees bring the queen food and care for her. The colony also has a few male bees. They are called *drones*. Their only job is to mate with the queen. After mating, the drones either die or are driven out of the colony.

This picture shows a honeybee queen and her workers. ⇒
You can see how much bigger she is than the other bees.

How Do Colonies Form?

In late spring or early summer, a queen bee lays some of her eggs in special, peanut-shaped combs. These combs are larger than the others. The workers take extra good care these eggs. That is because each of these eggs will grow up to be queen bees.

Since each colony can have only one queen, the old queen must leave. She gathers a large group of workers and sets out to find a new place to live. As they fly, the workers surround the queen to keep her safe. This large group is called a **swarm**. When the swarm finds a good place to build a hive, they form a new colony.

Back in the old colony, the new queens hatch from their eggs. The first queen to leave her comb quickly destroys all the other queen combs to make sure she is the only queen. She is the new queen of her own colony.

This swarm of honeybees is looking for a ⇒ new place to build their hive. Their queen is well protected in the center of the swarm.

Most bees drink nectar and eat a dust that flowers make called **pollen**. The flowers use pollen when they make seeds. Honeybees and bumblebees store nectar in their hives. If they store nectar too long, it spoils. To keep this from happening, the bees add special materials called *enzymes* to the nectar. The bees make the enzymes in their bodies. After a while, the enzymes turn the nectar into honey.

⇐ These honeybees are placing nectar in combs. You can see honey in the other combs around them.

How Do Honeybees Communicate?

Honeybees communicate in several different ways. They produce special smells to get other bees to work or to fight. A queen gives off smells that attract mates and order workers to care for her. Honeybees tell each other where to find food by doing a special "bee dance." The length of the dance and its speed tells other bees how far away the food is.

⇐ The bee in the middle of this picture is dancing to tell the other bees where to find nectar.

Are Bees Important?

Bees are important because they help plants to grow. Flowers need to have their pollen moved to a special part of the plant, or they can't make seeds. As bees fly from flower to flower searching for food, the pollen sticks to their body hairs. As they visit other flowers, they move the pollen to the special areas of the plants. This process is called **pollination**.

Top: This honeybee is collecting pollen from a flower. ⇒
Pollen from other flowers is stuck to the bee's legs.

Bottom: Next to a penny, you can see how big these pollen "baskets" are. They have been taken from of the legs of honeybees.

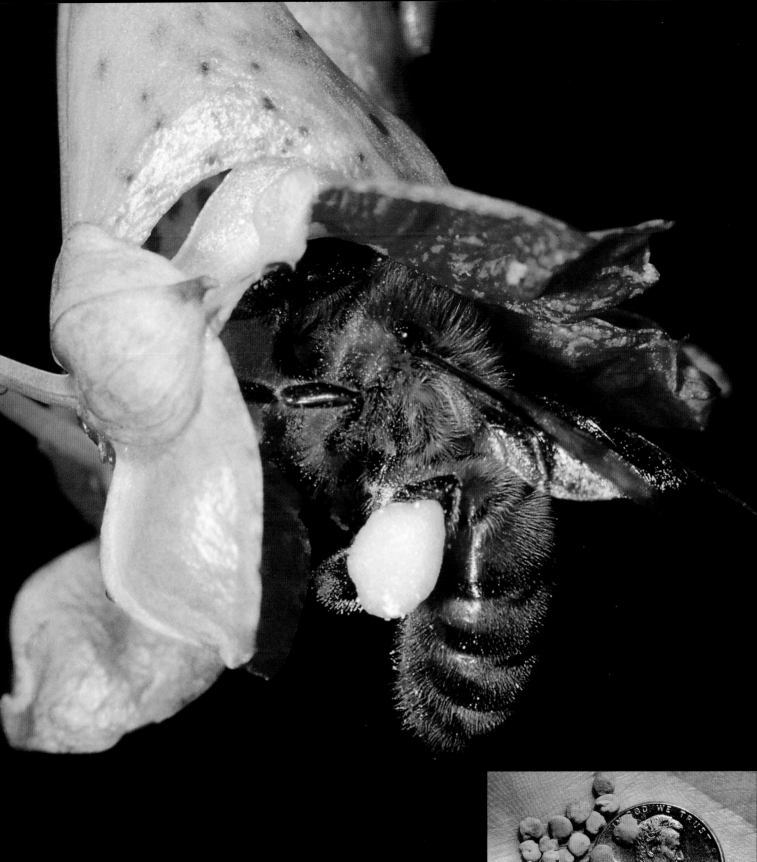

Many insects help in pollination, but bees are the most important. Without bees, flowering plants, trees and shrubs would not be able to make more plants. Some farmers and orchard owners even keep hives of honeybees to help pollinate their trees and crops.

Honey is also an important food for many people. People have been raising bees for honey for more than 4,000 years. So when you add some honey to your sandwich or cereal, say "thank you" to the bees!

Glossary

abdomen (AB-doh-men)
An insect's abdomen is its stomach area. Bees have a large abdomen.

barbs (BARBZ)
A barb is a sharp point or hook that sticks out from something. A honeybee's stinger has barbs.

colony (KOL-uh-nee)
A colony is a large group of insects that live together. Honeybees live in colonies.

combs (KOHMZ)
Bees make small rooms called combs in their hives. They use the combs for raising babies and storing food.

hives (HYVZ)
Large colonies of bees live in structures called hives. Hives are made up of many smaller rooms called combs.

insect (IN-sekt)
An insect is an animal with six legs, a body divided into three different areas, and usually one or two pairs of wings. Bees are insects.

nectar (NEK-ter)
Nectar is a sweet liquid that flowers make. Bees drink nectar and also make it into honey.

pollen (POL-len)
Pollen is a dust that flowers make to produce seeds. Many bees eat pollen.

pollination (pol-len-AY-shun)
Pollination is the process of moving pollen to the right areas of plants. Bees help in pollination when they are searching for food.

species (SPEE-sheez)
A species is a different kind of an animal. There are many different species of bees.

swarm (SWARM)
A swarm is a large, buzzing ball of bees. A queen bee and many workers swarm together when they are looking for a new colony.

thorax (THOR-aks)
The thorax is the chest area of an insect.

Web Sites

Visit our homepage for lots of links about bees!
http://www.childsworld.com/links.html

Note to Parents, Teachers, and Librarians:
We routinely verify our Web links to make sure they're safe, active sites—so encourage your readers to check them out!

Index